D1635589

" Do not fear,
for I have
redeemed you;
I have called
you by name,
you are mine. "

Isaiah 43:1

On most Methodist publications you will find the heraldic device of the Orb and Cross. It is not just a logo to 'brand' the Methodist Church, but has been carefully chosen to express our deepest beliefs.

The Orb represents the world, and the colour red (the traditional colour of Pentecost) may be taken to symbolise the Methodist conviction that through the power of the Holy Spirit all humanity may be saved.

The Orb is charged with a radiant Cross, which, like the field it is set on, is white, celebrating the glory of the risen Saviour. There is no boundary to the arms of the cross, just as there are no limits to the grace of God.

Ours is a faith that addresses the deepest longings of the heart, but it is always turned outwards to the world and its needs.

Contents

Introduction

> *A part of the church where I found my spiritual home.*

A Methodist member

To be a member of the Methodist Church is to play your full part in a huge, worldwide community.

We are part of the universal Church of Christ, bringing, as Methodists, our own special witness within it.

You may be considering becoming a member, or you may have been a member for some time, and want to think through what membership means. Perhaps you have recently joined a Methodist church, having previously worshipped in another church, or you are part of a Local Ecumenical Partnership (LEP), and want to know what is distinctive about Methodism.

This booklet does not stand alone. In order to get a fuller picture of what it means to be a Methodist, you will need:

Your local Methodist church

You can't be a Methodist member without belonging to a local Methodist church (or LEP). Everyone's membership is 'held' in a particular community of Christians (with all its joys and frustrations). It is the place where we are grounded in the basic teachings of the Christian faith, and where we try to help each other live these out.

The Bible

The teachings of the Methodist Church are based on the revelation of God recorded in the Bible. There are many different translations of the Bible, and many 'ways in', to help us apply the Bible to our daily lives.

Hymns & Psalms

It has been said that Methodism was 'born in song'. The hymns of Charles Wesley and others have helped generations of Methodists to learn and sing our faith. *Hymns & Psalms* is the most recent Methodist hymn book, but Methodists use good modern hymns and songs from other sources too.

The Methodist Worship Book

Methodist preachers and worship leaders do not have to use 'set' services, but the liturgies in the worship book are commonly used, and they embody what Methodists believe. You can find the service of 'Confirmation and Reception into Membership' here.

A Catechism for the use of the people called Methodists

This booklet includes statements agreed officially by the Methodist Church about key Christian beliefs, along with Bible passages which support them. These include the same core beliefs that are held by all Christians.

Worldwide, about 70 million people have links with the Methodist Church.

No longer my own -

You don't do this to be part of a club, but to be active in bringing healing and new life to the world.

A Methodist minister

In fact, Methodism did start as a kind of club. In the eighteenth century, a group of friends in Oxford met regularly for Bible study, prayer and Holy Communion, and they visited prisons and workhouses. One of them was John Wesley, an Anglican clergyman. He started the movement, organised into local religious gatherings or societies, that eventually became the Methodist Church.

The name 'Methodist' was first used as an insult – people thought Wesley and his followers took the gospel much too seriously. Rather than going to church just out of habit, Methodists have always believed that religion should come truly from the heart, and make a difference to how we live our lives. Traditionally, Methodists seek some 'method' of making sure that happens, for example by finding time to pray each day.

John Wesley prepared a special Covenant service, which Methodists still celebrate annually, usually at the new year. In it, members dedicate themselves once again to undertake the huge demands of the gospel, and enter into a covenant or solemn agreement with God.

Some people who are considering membership in the Methodist Church worry because they feel 'unworthy'. What the Covenant Prayer makes clear is that no-one is ever truly 'worthy' (the undertaking is so huge). But the grace of God is large enough to accept us as we are and transform what we offer into healing and life for the world.

the call to commitment

I am no longer my own but yours.

Put me to what you will,

rank me with whom you will;

put me to doing,

put me to suffering;

let me be employed for you,

or laid aside for you,

exalted for you,

or brought low for you;

let me be full,

let me be empty,

let me have all things,

let me have nothing:

I freely and wholeheartedly yield all things

to your pleasure and disposal.

And now, glorious and blessed God,

Father, Son and Holy Spirit,

you are mine and I am yours.

Covenant Prayer

All need to be saved.
All may be saved.
All may know themselves saved.
All may be saved to the uttermost.

Methodists have always been clear that no-one is beyond the reach of God's love. Salvation is there for everyone who turns to God, and not just for a chosen few.

As human beings we find ourselves part of an unjust, sinful and violent world which we may feel individually helpless to change. We may feel driven by urges such as anger, lust or greed, that we wish did not control us. We may have personalities which are difficult to manage, for instance being prone to despair. We may be enduring poverty and hardship.

The demands of modern life leave many of us stressed and overloaded, or isolated and feeling useless. Loss, fear, grief or guilt may be weighing us down. We need salvation.

Jesus preached the good news ('gospel') of the kingdom of God. At the same time he healed people, including those who were seen as being possessed by evil spirits. Through Jesus' death on the cross, and his resurrection, Christians believe that God has broken the power of all that is evil, in the world and in ourselves. If we accept forgiveness and liberation, and are willing to be open to the Holy Spirit, God can enable us to resist evil and to live life to the full, in this world and the next.

> Do you turn away from evil and all that denies God?
> By the grace of God, I do.
> Do you turn to God,
> trusting in Jesus Christ as Lord and Saviour,
> and in the Holy Spirit as Helper and Guide?
> By the grace of God, I do.
>
> Affirmation of faith made by candidates for membership

salvation for all

The Kingdom of God
Is justice and joy,
For Jesus restores
What sin would destroy.

Bryn Rees

In this depiction of the crucifixion, by Haitian artist Jacques Chéry, Christ's cross is also a tree of life, bearing resurrection fruit. Beneath his feet are contemporary powers of evil, and his arms encompass the rule of law, harmonious relationships, and a feast for hungry children.

And when human hearts
are breaking
Under sorrow's iron rod,
Then they find that
selfsame aching
Deep within the heart
of God.

Timothy Rees

> In the evening I went very unwillingly to a society at Aldersgate Street, where one was reading Luther's preface to the Epistle to the Romans. About a quarter before nine, while he was describing the change that God works in the heart through faith in Christ, I felt my heart strangely warmed. I felt I did trust in Christ, Christ alone, for salvation. And an assurance was given me that he had taken away <u>my</u> sins, even <u>mine</u>, and saved <u>me</u> from the law of sin and death.

John Wesley's journal

Epstein's sculpture of Lazarus emerging from the tomb (John 11) conveys a sense of someone still reluctant to encounter the light, yet wanting to come into Jesus' presence.

seeking assurance

John Wesley wrestled with difficult feelings on his journey of faith. Although already an ordained minister, he himself did not feel that he was truly loved and forgiven by God until the moment described in his journal. Indeed, he had wondered whether he should go on preaching. But he was given some wise advice: "Preach faith *till* you have it; and then, *because* you have it, you *will* preach faith."

If we have mixed feelings about our faith, or are unsure about whether we are feeling the 'right things', or unable to get away from feelings of guilt, it is encouraging to know that we are not alone in this. John Wesley did not give up on his search – he actually did go and listen, even if he went 'very unwillingly'. He put himself in the right place, and found that he was given the sense of joy and assurance he was looking for.

We do not have to wait until we 'have all the answers' before we can commit ourselves to membership of the Church. Our faith rests not on our subjective feelings, but on the promises of a faithful God.

Just as I am,
though tossed about
With many a conflict,
many a doubt,
Fightings and fears
within, without,
O Lamb of God, I come!

Charlotte Elliott

There is therefore now no condemnation for those who are in Christ Jesus.

Romans 8:1

"The hand with which I hold God is a trembling hand indeed, but the hand with which he holds me will never let me go."

Kingsley Barrett

Really meaning it -

Almighty God,
to whom all
hearts are
open,
all desires
known,
and from whom
no secrets are
hidden:
cleanse the
thoughts of our
hearts
by the
inspiration of
your Holy
Spirit,
that we may
perfectly love
you,
and worthily
magnify your
holy Name;
through Christ
our Lord.
Amen.

Collect for purity

This prayer, which has been prayed at the beginning of the Holy Communion service for centuries, speaks about our desire to love God 'perfectly'. Methodists have traditionally considered Christian 'perfection' and 'holiness' as being both desirable and possible.

This does not mean that we are to be driven and perfectionist, or think we are 'holier than thou'. Only God is absolutely perfect. After we have made a commitment, we will continue to make mistakes and to be tempted. It is about what we set our hearts on. 'Perfect love' (Christ-like love) is possible, if we completely depend on Christ. We are enabled to show God's love to others without our own selfishness getting in the way.

> Will you commit yourself to the Christian life of worship and service, and be open to the renewing power of God?
> With God's help I will.
> Will you seek the strength of God's Spirit as you accept the cost of following Jesus Christ in your daily life?
> With God's help I will.
> Will you witness, by word and deed, to the good news of God in Christ, and so bring glory to God?
> With God's help I will.
>
> Promises made by candidates for membership

There is no limit to what the Holy Spirit can accomplish in the lives of those who are totally consecrated to Christ.

An Anglican-Methodist Covenant

The fruit of the Spirit is love, joy, peace, patience, kindness, generosity, faithfulness, gentleness, and self-control.

Galatians 5:22

Refiner's fire
My heart's one desire
Is to be holy...

Brian Doerksen © 1990
Mercy/Vineyard Publishing/Copy
Care

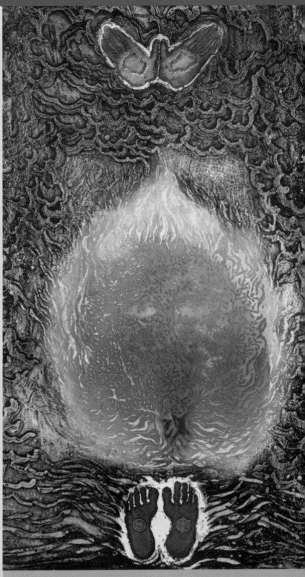

The Indian artist Paul Koli has conveyed a sense of the holiness of the presence of God in his depiction of the burning bush seen by Moses in the desert (Exodus 3).

He bids us build each other up;
And, gathered into one,
To our high calling's glorious hope
We hand in hand go on.

Charles Wesley

When those who are being received into membership have made their promises, the minister turns to the congregation and asks them to give their support as 'members of the body of Christ'.

The image of the Church as 'the body of Christ' dates back to St Paul, who worked to establish some of the earliest Christian communities. Just as a human body contains different but interdependent organs, so we should be close and caring enough to feel each other's pain and delight. We should put the good of the whole body before our own individual needs.

The promise of mutual support is a strength of Methodism. When you become a member, a pastoral visitor or a class leader is responsible for visiting you and offering spiritual support, encouragement and challenge.

Being a member of the Methodist Church means that you can hold certain offices or represent your church at the circuit meeting, the district synod or the Conference (see pp. 16-17). No-one should put pressure on you to take on any responsibility you do not feel ready for. But as part of the body, you will have your own gifts to offer, and it is important to discover what these are, and use them - in the Church and in the world.

Other Christians may sometimes be difficult for us to work with and to love. John Wesley gives some realistic advice in his *Plain Account of Christian Perfection:*

> Do not allow yourself one thought of separating from your brothers and sisters, whether their opinions agree with yours or not. Do not dream that anyone sins in not believing you, in not taking your word......Oh, beware of touchiness, of testiness.....expect contradiction and opposition..... Receive them from people with humility, meekness, yieldingness, gentleness, sweetness.

Being connected -

> *The Gospel of Christ knows no religion but social; no holiness but social holiness.*
>
> John Wesley

'Holiness' is not achieved except in community. Methodism has a strong sense of community, which is expressed in the way it is organised. It calls itself a **Connexion**.

No local church operates alone. It is usually part of a group of churches, the **Circuit**. A number of circuits make up a **District** – there are 33 in the British Methodist Church. Like all other levels of the Church, Districts are responsible to the **Methodist Conference**. Representatives of all Districts attend this governing body which meets annually, hosted in different locations each year. This is where Methodist doctrine and policy are agreed and adopted. Conference is led by an elected **President** (always a presbyter) and a **Vice-President** (a lay person or deacon). They travel around the Connexion on behalf of the Conference during their year of office.

This collaborative structure is important to Methodist belief. We believe that the 'whole people of God' shares the same calling. Ordained ministers do not have a calling that is different in kind from the rest of God's people. British Methodism has two kinds of ordained minister. **Presbyters** (normally called 'ministers') preach, preside at Holy Communion, and have pastoral responsibility for congregations. **Deacons**, who are members of a religious order, have a ministry of service, often of a specialised nature.

Lay leadership is a great strength of Methodism. Most of the leading of worship and preaching is done by **Local Preachers**, who have been specially trained. Every presbyter started off as a local preacher. Many important responsibilities are held by lay people, including various **Stewards**, who share in guiding the life of the local church or circuit.

the Connexion

Some churches, circuits and districts employ **Lay Workers** and **Youth Workers**.

The **Methodist Council** meets throughout the year to guide the Church between Conferences. The **Connexional Team** resources the Church in carrying out what Conference has agreed.

> Connexionalism is a Methodist vision of how to live together well.....It is an extension of the idea of friendship. Every group, association, institution and community is connected to every other one.
>
> David Deeks

At Conference, before their ordination, both presbyters and deacons are formally '**received into full Connexion**'. All deacons and most presbyters are **itinerant**, which means that they are sent by Conference to work wherever they are needed. Most are appointed to a circuit, and some to work out their ministry in the secular world.

Our Calling, in the Methodist Church in Britain, is to:

increase **awareness** of **God's presence** and to celebrate **God's love**

help people to **grow** and **learn** as **Christians** through mutual support and care

be a good **neighbour** to people in **need** and to **challenge injustice**

make **more followers** of **Jesus Christ**

Every member of the Methodist Church receives a 'ticket' of membership at least once a year. This is signed by our minister and tells us who our pastoral visitor or class leader is.

Some members keep the card in their purse or wallet, others put it on their mantelpiece or use it as a bookmark in their Bible. It is not an 'entry ticket', but a reminder of our identity as a Methodist, and of the commitments we have taken on.

The annual ticket includes an explanation of these commitments.

To serve the present age,
My calling to fulfil; -
O may it all my powers engage
To do my Master's will!

Charles Wesley

As a member of the Methodist Church I am called to:

worship within the local church, including regular sharing in Holy Communion, and through personal prayer

learning and caring, through Bible study and meeting for fellowship, so that I may grow in faith and support others in their discipleship

service, by being a good neighbour in the community, challenging injustice and using my resources to support the Church in its mission in the world

evangelism, through working out my faith in daily life and sharing Christ with others.

Public Worship

The most important reason for going to church along with other Christians is to worship God. Many people develop a deep love for the familiar church building they worship in. But it is the gathering of people, the 'body of Christ' who are the church. Methodism welcomes and values everyone who wants to come and be a part of public worship.

Methodist services are led by a minister, a local preacher or a worship leader. The style of a service can range from formal to very informal or experimental. It depends on those leading worship and on the practice of the local church. However, all acts of worship are likely to include the following elements:

● **Preparation** - a time to help us gather in God's presence, offer prayers of adoration, confess our sins and have an assurance of forgiveness

● **Ministry of the Word** - including Bible readings and a way of reflecting on what we have heard (usually a sermon)

● **Response** - a time of thanksgiving, of prayer for the world and for each other, and dedication of ourselves and our gifts

● **Dismissal** - when we are blessed and sent out into the world.

Holy Communion

Some services include Holy Communion. Anyone, of any age, who has been baptised is welcome to receive bread and wine. Church members are particularly encouraged to come regularly.

Holy Communion is also called the Lord's Supper, because it recalls Jesus' last supper with his friends on the night before he was crucified. We believe that as we eat the bread and drink the wine, through the power of the Holy Spirit we receive our Lord by faith, with thanksgiving.

The 'wine' in a Methodist church is non-alcoholic. Although individual Methodists have freedom of conscience to drink alcohol, the Church as a whole recognises that alcohol can destroy lives and that there should be places where those who are vulnerable to it are protected.

You shall love the Lord your God with all your heart, and with all your soul, and with all your mind, and with all your strength.

Mark 12:30

Jacques Iselin's rich painting explores through colour and symbolism the mystery of Holy Communion. The elements of bread and wine are there, and the fish is an ancient symbol of Christ himself, present with us.

Celebrate God's love -

Be still, for the presence of the Lord,
the Holy One, is here.
Come bow before him now with reverence and fear.
In him no sin is found,
we stand on holy ground.

Extract taken from the song 'Be still' by David J Evans. © 1986 Thankyou Music.

Wherever we are consciously in the presence of God, we are on 'holy ground'. In one way, prayer is 'natural'. It is the communication, spoken or unspoken, that builds the relationship between ourselves and God. But in another way, it is difficult to do because it is fearful to come into the presence of the living God. We would usually prefer to follow any distraction rather than 'be still' in God's presence. Many Christians struggle with prayer, and it can help to have a structured way or time set aside. This time of stillness can then affect all the rest of what we do.

The Methodist Church produces a Prayer Handbook each year. This gives a pattern of Bible readings and a hymn to meditate on for every day in the year, and specific prayers for each day of the month. It includes topics for prayer from the Methodist Church worldwide, and the 33 Districts in the Connexion. Using the handbook, we can pray alone, knowing that many others are praying with us and following the same themes.

Many churches have special prayer meetings, and most people find their own prayer life deepened by praying with others regularly.

personal prayer

Nathaniel comes to Jesus, who recognises him, saying 'I saw you under the fig tree'. (John 1). The artist Mark Cazalet here shows Nathaniel asleep but naked under the tree. It is as if Jesus has seen and understood him completely - nothing is hidden. This is a good, if unusual, image of prayer. It shows someone resting under God's gaze, totally exposed, totally trusting.

> All that Christians do, even in eating and sleeping, is prayer when done in simplicity, according to the order of God.....Prayer continues in the desire of the heart, though the understanding be employed on outward things.
>
> John Wesley

Roy de Maistre shows the moment during the story of the walk to Emmaus (Luke 24), when the two disciples suddenly recognise the risen Jesus as he breaks bread with them. They said to each other, *"Were not our hearts burning within us while he was talking to us on the road, while he was opening the scriptures to us?"*

another in love

"

A society is no other than a company of persons having the form and seeking the power of godliness, united in order to pray together, to receive the word of exhortation, and to watch over one another in love that they may help each other to work out their salvation.

John Wesley

Perhaps the greatest strength of early Methodism was its emphasis on the power of the small group of committed Christians to love, support and challenge each other on their journeys of faith. Every member belonged to a class meeting. These met every week, and everyone was encouraged to be open and accountable to each other about how far they were truly living the Christian life.

In recent years many churches have rediscovered the importance of small groups meeting regularly (often in someone's home), for prayer, Bible study, and discussion.

All of us need to learn and grow in our understanding of our faith, and our faith is likely to change and develop during the course of our lives as we deepen in maturity. Major life experiences will have an impact on how we relate to our faith, and we need support to help us reflect on these. The companionship of other Christians whom we have come to trust is one of the most important ways for us to understand the working of God's grace in our lives.

Each heart's deep instinct unconfessed;
Each lowly wish, each daring claim;
All, all that life has long repressed
Unfolds, undreading blight or blame.

Dora Greenwell

- the call to learn

Applying our faith

A living faith is always one which is applied to real life. It isn't just a set of beliefs which we have learned about or agree with in principle. We aren't given blueprints for how to behave in every situation or dilemma we face.

Methodists traditionally use a four-fold approach to apply our Christian faith to contemporary issues and to our Christian practice:

Scripture

We seek to discover the Word of God through 'searching the scriptures'. There are different understandings among Methodists about the Bible's authority in our lives. We need to use resources like different Bible translations, commentaries, and Bible reading notes.

Reason

We are called to love God with our minds as well as with our hearts. To the best of our ability we need to think things through in the light of reason. This means becoming aware of different points of view (for example by reading), and using our own critical thinking in order to make sense of God's world.

Tradition

This is the wisdom and creativity of Christians over time and all across the world. It includes inspirational material like hymns and songs, prayers, poetry, Christian art and devotional books, as well as formally agreed teachings like the creeds, the contents of the catechism, and statements and reports from the Methodist Conference.

Experience

Methodism in particular has stressed the importance of our own experience of the grace of God working in our lives. We gain wisdom and maturity from life experience (including our feelings, gut reactions and intuitions), especially when we have prayed and reflected about our story with other Christians.

and care

For the majority of Methodists, **Scripture** carries the most weight. For some, **Experience** is a compelling 'way in'. But all four resources need to be used together as we work out our faith. To ignore any of these approaches is going to leave us unbalanced and immature as Christians.

© Colin Barratt

> Neither the learned nor the unlearned are saved from the trouble of thinking. All are to think. This is the way to understand the things of God. Meditate day and night.
>
> From *John Wesley's Message Today*

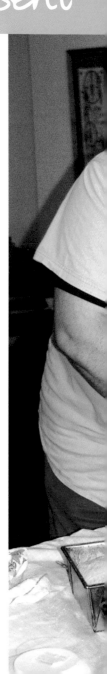

> Since God is invisible to our eyes, we are to serve God in our neighbour, which God receives as if done to himself in person, standing visibly before us.
>
> John Wesley

Methodism has always combined a focus on the individual response to God with a passionate and active concern for social justice. The huge crowds who heard and responded to Wesley's preaching were often the poor. The upper classes regarded him as a threat to the social order because he treated the lower classes as equally human. Early Methodists were active in the struggle against slavery, campaigned for prison reform and set up a range of educational initiatives to improve literacy and health as well as to develop understanding in the faith. Contemporary Methodist charities like NCH and Methodist Homes are part of this tradition of practical caring for young and old in society.

In recent times, the Methodist Church has been fully engaged, with other Churches and those of other faiths or none, in challenging injustice in our contemporary world. Examples of these are racism and sexism, human rights abuses, unfair trading practices, unethical investment, environmental pollution and Third World debt.

Our Christianity is never for ourselves alone. Methodist members are called to care for our own household and church community, but also to go well beyond these bounds in showing God's care for the world.

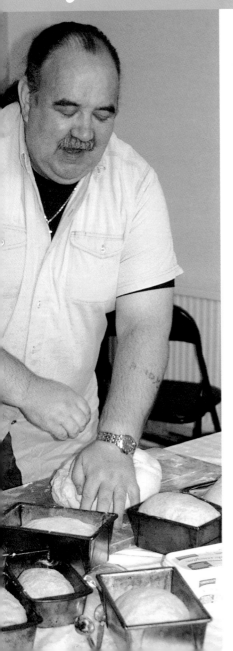

Sent by the Lord am I;
my hands are ready now
to make the earth the place
in which the Kingdom comes.
The angels cannot change
a world of hurt and pain
into a world of love,
of justice and of peace.
The task is mine to do ...

Traditional Nicaraguan song

Methodists in Liverpool City Centre have no church building any more, but they have a ministry of making bread and sharing it with all who visit their rented premises, above a bookshop called 'News from Nowhere'.

Sieger Köder shows Jesus humbly kneeling before Peter, washing his feet (see John 13). Jesus' face is seen reflected in the murky water of the basin. His own bare feet look vulnerable too.

This is our God, the Servant King,
he calls us now to follow him,
to bring our lives as a daily offering
of worship to the Servant King.

Extract taken from the song 'The Servant King' by Graham Kendrick. Copyright © 1983 Thankyou Music

> What does the Lord require of you but to do justice, and to love kindness, and to walk humbly with your God?

Micah 6:8

Being a good neighbour

Jesus' story of the sheep and the goats in Matthew 25 makes it clear that we encounter God face to face when we respond to those who are in need. We are expected to offer our time, our compassion, and the practical work of our hands. It means considering what paid work or voluntary action God may be calling us to do.

Challenging injustice

Christians sometimes behave as if we have been called to be 'nice', rather than to witness to the truth. Jesus was outspoken in challenging what he saw as wrong in his society and religion. Luke 4:14-19 sets out his priorities – to bring good news and freedom to those who are poor, imprisoned, and oppressed.

Using our resources to support the Church in its mission

Our financial resources, together with our time and talents, are held by us in trust from God. Wesley's attitude to giving was very demanding. He thought that after supplying our own 'reasonable wants' and those of our family, *all* the rest of our money should be given to God through the poor. In a culture where we are urged to spend and consume continually, the Christian alternative is to give in proportion to what God has given us. One way of thinking about this seriously is to compare what we spend on leisure activities with what we give for the Church's mission in the world.

> Those who do not love a brother or sister whom they have seen, cannot love God whom they have not seen.

1 John 4:20

Making more followers

The call to evangelism

> The world hears the gospel when it sees it.
>
> Albert Outler

Human beings naturally want to share good news, and Christians who sense the joy and power of God in their lives are no exception. But some people feel anxious about a responsibility to 'evangelise'. Perhaps we do not want to put pressure on other people to believe that we are right, or imply that their view of the world is invalid. Methodists respect people of other faiths and alternative spiritualities, and are encouraged to be in dialogue with them.

The most eloquent witness to the gospel will be the kind of life we lead. However, other people can, understandably, be irritated by those of us who go to church, but can't actually say what it is we stand for.

Evangelism is not about collaring some reluctant person and demanding to know if they are 'saved'. It is simply about being willing to 'give a reason for the faith that is in us' at the right time – about telling our story, sharing our journey. Of course, if we never give the time to reflecting on this with other supportive Christians, it is most unlikely that we shall have the confidence (or find the right words) to share it with someone who might challenge what we say.

To speak openly about the things that matter most to us is going to make us feel vulnerable. No-one ever suggested that the Christian life was going to be easy. But we can all be a 'means of grace' for others, we can all sometimes speak the Word of God by finding the right words at the right time. Someone has done that for us, or we wouldn't be here on this journey. Now it's our turn.

> For I handed on to you as of the first importance what I in turn had received....
>
> 1 Corinthians 15:3

Will you come
and follow me
if I but call
your name?

Will you go
where you
don't know
and never be
the same?

Will you let
my love be
shown,

will you let
my name be
known,

will you let
my life be
grown
in you and
you in me?

John Bell and Graham Maule

George Nene depicts the risen Christ appearing to the women and sending them to tell the good news of the resurrection (see Matthew 28).

'Bleib Sein Kind', Dorothea Steigerwald

God is with us.

"I am convinced that neither death, nor life, nor angels, nor rulers, nor things present, nor things to come, nor powers, nor height, nor depth, nor anything else in all creation, will be able to separate us from the love of God in Christ Jesus our Lord."

Romans 8:38-39

Resources

Bible – a good modern translation such as New Revised Standard Version (NRSV), Revised English Bible (REB), New Century Version or New International Version (NIV).

Hymns & Psalms – the hymnbook of the Methodist Church

A modern hymnbook such as *Mission Praise, Songs of Fellowship, Let's Praise, Common Ground.*

The Methodist Worship Book

A Catechism for the use of people called Methodists

The Methodist Prayer Handbook – published annually. Available from the Methodist Bookshop, Methodist Church House or Methodist Publishing House.

Flame – the Methodist Magazine – a bi-monthly magazine celebrating what it means to be Christian in the Methodist tradition. To subscribe, contact Methodist Publishing House.

Magnet – the magazine of Women's Network – available from your local church or circuit distributor. Details from the Women's Network Office, Methodist Church House.

The Connexional Link Mailing providing information, resources and encouragement for churches, sent to every Methodist church and every Methodist minister. Also available from Methodist Publishing House, four times a year.

The Methodist Website – www.methodist.org.uk

The Methodist Recorder – available weekly from your newsagent or by subscription from 122 Golden Lane, London EC1Y 0TL.

The Methodist Resources Catalogue – published annually. This includes a wealth of material including Bible reading notes, study notes, devotional material, and books covering a wide range of Methodist and Christian life. Available from Methodist Publishing House.

Useful addresses

Methodist Church House
(including the Methodist Bookshop)
25 Marylebone Road, London,
NW1 5JR
Tel: 020 7486 5502

Methodist Publishing House
4 John Wesley Road, Werrington,
Peterborough PE4 6ZP
Tel: 01733 325002
Fax: 01733 384180
www.mph.org.uk
E-mail: sales@mph.org.uk

To discover more about the meaning of membership in the Methodist Church, or to find out practical details about membership preparation in your local church, talk to your minister.

Acknowledgements

The material in this book has been prepared by Janet Morley on behalf of the Methodist Church, with help from Ken Kingston, and in consultation with the Faith and Order Committee of the Methodist Church and many others.

Quotations

Page

1
- Isaiah 43:1, *New Revised Standard Version of the Bible (NRSV)*.

4
- Methodist member, survey by Susan Johnson (2000), on 'what does it mean to you to belong to the Methodist Church?'

6
- Methodist minister, survey by Janet Morley (2001) of ministers successfully making new members.

7
- From the Covenant Prayer based on the words of John Wesley, *Methodist Worship Book (MWB)*, p. 290. A modern version is also included, pp. 288-289.

8
- Traditional summary of Methodist teaching, para. 68, *A Catechism for the use of the people called Methodists*.
- Questions put to candidates in the Service of Confirmation and Reception into Membership, *MWB*, pp. 98-99.

9
- *Hymns & Psalms (H&P)* 139, v. 1, Bryn Rees. Used by permission.
- *H&P* 36, v. 2, 'God is Love: let heaven adore him' by Timothy Rees, reproduced with permission of Continuum Publishing Ltd.

10
- From John Wesley's journal, 24 May 1738.

11
- Advice given by Peter Böhler, a German Moravian pastor.
- *H&P 697*, v. 2, Charlotte Elliott.
- Romans 8:1, *NRSV*.
- Rev Kingsley Barrett, address to the Methodist Conference 1973.

12
- *MWB*, p. 185.
- Promises made by the candidates in the Service of Confirmation and Reception into Membership, *MWB*, p. 101.

13
- *An Anglican-Methodist Covenant*, para. 120, p. 39.
- Galatians 5:22, *NRSV*.
- 'Refiner's Fire' by Brian Doerksen, copyright © 1990 Mercy/Vineyard Publishing administered by CopyCare PO Box 77, Hailsham, BN27 3EF music@copycare.com. Used by permission.

14
- *H&P 753*, v. 2, Charles Wesley.
- Promise by the congregation in the Service of Confirmation and Reception into Membership, *MWB*, p. 101.

15
- John Wesley, *A Plain Account of Christian Perfection*.

16
- John Wesley, *A Plain Account of Christian Perfection*.

17
- Rev David Deeks, Co-ordinating Secretary for Church and Society in the Connexional Team.

18 • *Our Calling*, adopted by the
    Methodist Conference 2000.
19 • *H&P 785*, v. 2, Charles Wesley.
    • Commitments of membership,
    adopted by the Methodist Conference
    2002.
21 • Mark 12:30, *NRSV*.
22 • 'Be still' by David J. Evans. ©
    copyright 1986 Thankyou Music, adm.
    by worshiptogether.com songs excl. UK
    & Europe, adm. by Kingsway Music.
    tym@kingsway.co.uk. Used by
    permission.
23 • John Wesley, *A Plain Account of
    Christian Perfection*.
24 • Luke 24:32, *NRSV*.
25 • John Wesley, 'The Rules of the
    United Societies', *The Constitutional
    Practice and Discipline of the
    Methodist Church (volume 1)*.
    • *H&P 415*, v. 3, Dora Greenwell.
27 • Lovett H. Weems Jr, *John Wesley's
    Message Today* (Nashville, Abingdon
    Press, 1982)
28 • John Wesley, *A Plain Account of
    Christian Perfection*.
29 • 'Sent by the Lord' from *Sent by the
    Lord* (Glasgow, Wild Goose
    Publications, 1991). Translated by
    Jorge Maldonado © public domain.
30 • 'The Servant King' by Graham
    Kendrick © 1983 Thankyou Music,
    adm. by worshiptogether.com songs
    excl. UK & Europe, adm. by Kingsway
    Music. tym@kingsway.co.uk. Used by

    permission.
31 • Micah 6:8, *NRSV*.
    • 1 John 4:20, *NRSV*.
32 • Albert Outler, *Evangelism in the
    Wesleyan Spirit* (Nashville, Tidings,
    1971).
    • 1 Corinthians 15:3, NRSV.
33 • V. 1 of 'Will you come and follow me'
    from *Heaven shall not wait* (Glasgow,
    Wild Goose Publications, 1987).
    Words: John L. Bell and Graham Maule
    © 1987 WGRG, Iona Community,
    Glasgow G2 3DH.
34 • (banner) John Wesley, his dying
    words.
35 • Romans 8:38-39, *NRSV*.

Quotations from *The New Revised Standard
Version of the Bible* (Anglicized Edition) ©
1989, 1985, Division of Christian Education of
the National Council of the Churches of Christ
in the United States of America. Used by
permission. All rights reserved.

Quotations from T*he Methodist Worship Book*
(Peterborough, Methodist Publishing House,
1999), *A Catechism for the use of the people
called Methodists* (Peterborough, Methodist
Publishing House, 2000), *An Anglican-
Methodist Covenant* (Peterborough, Methodist
Publishing House, 2001), *Our Calling*
(Methodist Conference 2000), *Membership
Ticket* (Methodist Conference 2002), *The
Constitutional Practice and Discipline of the
Methodist Church* (volume 1) (Peterborough,

Methodist Publishing House, 1988) ©
Trustees for Methodist Church Purposes
(TMCP). Used by permission.

Images
We are grateful for the use of images from the Methodist Church Collection of Modern Christian Art:

Page

21 • 'The Elements of Holy Communion', Jacques Iselin (b. 1933), oil, 1963 © TMCP.

23 • 'Nathaniel (asleep under the fig tree)', Mark Cazalet (b. 1964), oil on paper, 1993 © TMCP.

24 • 'The supper at Emmaus', Roy de Maistre (1894-1968), oil, 1958 © TMCP (also cover image).

© Photographs: The Trustees of the Methodist Collection of Modern Christian Art.

Other images:

Page

4 • Photograph: Mark Howard/Twenty-Five Educational.

9 • Misereor Hunger Cloth from Haiti by Jacques Chéry. © 1982 Misereor Medienproduktion, Aachen.

10 • 'Lazarus', Sir Jacob Epstein (1880-1959), New College Chapel, Oxford © Tate, London 2002. Photograph: Oxfordshire County Council

Photographic Archive – Thomas Photos.

13 • 'The Burning Bush' by Paul Koli, India, from The Bible Through Asian Eyes, eds. Masao Takenako and Ron O'Grady (Pace Publishing - Auckland New Zealand, in association with the Asian Christian Art Association - Kyoto, Japan, 1991). Used by permission of the Asian Christian Art Association.

17 • Photograph: Paul Harrington/The Methodist Recorder.

27 • Elaine Coupe at The Methodist School of Fellowship 2001. Photograph: Colin Barratt.

28 • Andy Ross. Photograph: Audrey Parker.

30 • 'The Washing of Feet' © Sieger Köder, Fußwaschung.

33 • 'The Risen Christ reveals himself first to the Two Women', George Nene, Zimbabwe, in Welcome to Zimbabwe (Geneva, World Council of Churches, 1988). Copyright permission applied for.

34 • 'Bleib Sein Kind', Dorothea Steigerwald (b. 1918) © Brendow Verlag, D-47443 Moers. Photograph: Mark Howard/Twenty-Five Educational.